IN
UNDEI
AND BREAK FREE
FROM YOUR OWN
LIMITATIONS

MATTHEW BRIGHTHOUSE

TABLE OF CONTENTS

1 INTRODUCTION..3

2 THE FINE LINE BETWEEN STRENGTH AND WEAKNESS 7

3 LEARN HOW TO BE MORE SOCIALLY OPEN 14

4 LEARN HOW TO BE MORE SENSITIVE AND IN TOUCH WITH YOUR EMOTIONS 18

5 LEARN HOW TO BECOME MORE ORGANIZED AND PRESENT IN THE MOMENT 22

6 LEARN HOW TO BE MORE SECURE IN YOUR DECISIONS...26

7 LEARN HOW TO COMBINE PROBLEM SOLVING AND YOUR IMAGINATION 30

8 CONCLUSION 33

NOTE FROM THE AUTHOR 36

1
Introduction

If you have recently taken the Myers Briggs Personality Test and you have drawn the INTP type, this book is for you.

Every single personality type (all of them), have certain traits which make them stand out from the others on the list. These are positive elements, e.g. strengths, and there are negative elements, the weaknesses. The key to personality growth and personal fulfilment is to work on those prescribed negatives, and to turn them around to become strengths in the end.

Understanding your own personality is key to understanding who you are as a person. Despite your category of personality type, you are different from the other INTPs you may come across, because we all have our own personal quirks. This might mean that you display a key feature of the INTP personality type more than someone else, but then on another element, they are stronger towards that than you. The degree to which you are afflicted, or gifted, with the personality traits of an INTP really doesn't matter, what matters is that you turn them all around into positives, to further allow yourself to grow as a whole, well-rounded person.

Of course, we all have free will in terms of the decisions we make, or actions, and their coordinating consequences as a result, but our personality type traits really do influence a lot of the restrictions we place upon ourselves and our decisions on a daily basis.

An INTP personality type is a complicated kind of deal; you are someone who is not only fact-focused, driven, and highly determined, but you are also someone who has a tendency to shyness, and someone who can often fail to see the human or emotional side of things, whilst concentrating perhaps a little too much on logic or fact. You can also occasionally be a bit of a rebel, detesting rules or guidelines and their restrictions, but you are not someone who is overly confident about pushing yourself forward, tending to second guess everything for a minute too long on occasion.

This might all sound like a paradox, but that is what makes an INTP personality type so intriguing. There is a lot to work with here, and a lot of space for personal growth and fulfilment. Of course, there are many positives to being an INTP also, with a fantastic imagination, an enthusiastic nature, and you are also very open minded too, a very positive and forward-thinking trait to have.

So, how can you blend the best of your personality type, whilst also improving the so-called negatives? It's all about pinpointing the areas you need to work on, and to what degree. This book will give you all the information you need about your INTP personality type, and whilst you might not see a huge amount of yourself in some particular factors, remember that it is likely to be there, perhaps hidden a little under the surface. Allow yourself to use that open-minded trait to see a little outside of the box, and from there, you can learn to accept yourself wholly, and improve your perceived negativities.

Which is better, introversion or extraversion?

We should address this issue because there is a lot of debate about it. Whilst an extravert is usually much easier to approach and speak to, easier to engage with, and usually the life and soul of the party, is that always a good thing? If you are an introvert, you might be beating yourself up, because you're not loud, you're not always out there speaking to others, you're not grabbing every new opportunity that comes along, all loud and proud, but that shouldn't be something you are sad about.

An introvert is a cool, calm, and very logical person. Many of the world's most quietly successful people, e.g. businessmen and women, are introverts. Sometimes the ability to be quiet, listen, take everything in, and make logical decisions will get you much further than a louder or more 'out there' approach.

That's not to say that extraversion is a bad thing however, but the notion that introversion is somehow second in the queue needs to be abolished. We are what we are, and if you are an introvert, you should embrace that. You have a calmness, a sense of serenity, you can read people, you are intuitive without being over the top, and you can listen, really listen. The only possible downside is a potential for shyness, but that can be overcome, with a little help, advice, and hard work. So, which is better? Neither, they are both equal.

Now we have put that point to bed, are you ready to totally embrace your INTP self, all the good, bad, and the in-between? This journey is going to take some careful thinking, examination and decision making, but hey, that's what an INTP loves, right?

So, get yourself comfortable, turn off your phone, and let's begin!

2
The Fine Line Between Strength And Weakness

How do you really spell INTP? What does this rather confusing abbreviation really mean?

This chapter is going to tell you all you need to know about your strengths and weaknesses as an INTP personality type, before we move into further chapters on how to help you improve those weaknesses, and turn them into real strengths. From that point, there really will be no stopping you!

Every personality type that you will have found in the Myers Briggs test is a combination of four letters, and these are the main dominant traits of that particular personality type. You are an INTP.

So, what does INTP mean?

I = Introversion
N = Intuition
T = Thinking
P = Perceiving

As you can see, an INTP is quite a deep person, but their tendency to focus a little too much on logic rather than emotion can be a stumbling block. An INTP is known as the logical one, the highly intuitive and intelligent one. `

Let's look at each letter in turn.

Introversion

An INTP personality is not an outgoing soul, instead, you are likely to be much more comfortable with spending time alone, that's not to say that you are at all boring or antisocial, it's just that you joy getting so deep into things, that you often forget to engage with others! You are a real thinker, you are likely to be a dreamer to a degree, but not a dreamer who considers fairy-tale endings, instead you are more likely to be thinking about how things work, how you can jump your way over hurdles.

You are honest and you don't tend to deviate from the truth; basically, you say it how it is, and at times that can get you into trouble, because you can be a little too blunt, without really meaning to be.

You have a close circle of friends, rather than a large group, because your occasional tendency to be a tiny bit too straight-forward has the habit of rubbing people up the wrong way occasionally. Your close circle understands you, and love you for your 'no rubbish' way of thinking.

Intuition
Your creativity really helps develop your intuition, and you have a 'gut feeling' about most things. This helps you make logical decisions, rather than leaning too much on the 'dreamer' side of things. Logic and fact is your friend, despite your imaginative nature. Your imagination is therefore much more useful in terms of helping you solve problems, often in ways that some other people would never have thought of, and this helps you achieve great success.

As with anyone who relies upon their intuition, you can be subject to the occasional crisis of confidence, where you second guess your own decisions and even yourself from time to time. It is important for INTPs to develop greater confidence in their own being, to avoid delays when making important choices in life.

Thinking
Oh, you are a great thinker indeed! Coming up with creative answers to problems is truly your forte, but you also have the slight tendency to be a tad bit condescending when working as part of a team to solve an issue. This isn't something you intend to do by any means, but your drive and determination to solve the problem itself can often get in the way of someone else's feelings. Insensitivity is a key trait of an INTP personality type, but don't worry, we're not painting you as a terrible person! The key to bettering yourself is accepting the negatives and positives of your personality type, and by being more aware of how you are dealing with other people, especially when you are caught up in the moment, you can improve this potential downside, and turn it into something much more positive.

Your objective way of thinking means you are a fantastic person to have on a team when working on a project, because you are open minded to different solutions, and you don't let yourself become swayed by 'what if'... Despite that, we did mention that you can occasionally begin to second guess your own decisions if you allow yourself to ponder them too much, and this is also something to focus on.

Perceiving
Perceiving is a trait of an introverted personality type, which we know the INTP to be. You are displaying perceiving behavior when you are acting in a spontaneous manner, when you decide what you are going to do as you do it, without making a long-term plan first, but on the flipside, you can also be perceiving when you avoid making a firm decision, and instead prefer to explore your other options first. Most INTPs tend to leave things until the

very last minute until doing them, so if you find yourself a little unorganized, this can be your INTP traits coming out!

Perceiving isn't necessarily a negative however, because spontaneity is of course the spice of life, and whilst you are displaying perceiving behavior, you are avoiding the other possible negative of your personality type – dilly dallying on decisions and second guessing what you are going to do. Yes, INTPs can be complicated!

So, now we know what INTP stands for, you are probably seeing a lot more of yourself displayed in these descriptions. Are you feeling keen to learn more? That is the aim, because this means that you are open to improving the possible negatives and flipping it around. True personal growth occurs when we are open to change, when we can accept our flaws as well as our positives, and decide to work on them for overall growth and happiness in the future.

Let's sum up the main strengths and weaknesses of the INTP personality trait, to really display just how much of a fine line there is between the two.

Strengths of an INTP personality type

- Well-developed analysis skills – An INTP can analyze anything, to find a solution to the issue, as well as being fantastic at thinking outside of the box, to find much more creative solutions
- Fantastic imagination, yet logical – A logical imagination is what fuels the above point, the ability to find abstract answers to problems and questions
- Originality – An INTP has a quiet confidence about them; their introverted nature doesn't mean they are lacking on self-confidence, instead it means they have

a sense of self-assuredness about them, which means they don't need to copy anyone else

- Open minded nature – One of the most positive traits of an INTP is that they are very open minded about everything in life, and very accepting of diversity
- Excited and enthusiastic – When a task is at hand, an INTP can easily get their teeth right into it, and become very enthusiastic about working on it to a final solution. This means an INTP is a great person to have on a problem-solving team
- An ability to be objective – An INTP will be able to see all sides of an argument or issue, which allows them to assess the best way to solve it or deal with it
- Very honest, and tells it like it is – You could argue that this isn't necessarily always a good trait, but an INTP is always very honest, and doesn't sugar coat anything; they will literally tell you what they think, and occasionally this can be a tad insensitive – they don't mean it though!

Weaknesses of an INTP personality type

- Social shyness – Whilst an INTP is self-assured on the inside, they can sometimes find it hard to be chatty or open in social situations. A fierce sense of privacy can make them come across as being rather withdrawn, because they are always thinking inside their own head, rather than talking to those in their immediate surroundings
- Can be insensitive, without meaning to be – We have touched upon this a few times already, but the straight forward nature of an INTP personality type means that occasionally they can be a little insensitive to the emotions of others. Preferring to focus on fact

and logic rather than emotion, this can occasionally be an issue

- Can be forgetful – An INTP has the tendency to be a bit absent minded on occasion also, forgetful, and a little disorganized. They have a habit of becoming so drawn into their imaginations and problem solving, that everything else goes by the by
- Can also be condescending – Aside from the insensitivity issue, an INTP may condescend others when explaining something. Because they focus so much on logic, anyone who looks more on the side of feeling and emotion is not really understood by an INTP, and their approach to explain this can be lacking
- Really doesn't enjoy rules – The rebel side of the INTP means that guidelines and rules are not loved! Learning to respect the rules is something an INTP needs to work on
- Can be a little unsure of themselves – Second guessing decisions, despite being spontaneous with decision making, can be a complicated mixture.

As you can see, the strengths and weaknesses of the INTP personality type really do overlap a little, and that is the fine line we have been talking about. You should definitely celebrate your strengths, because they are great strengths to have, but over the coming chapters we are going to focus much more on the weaknesses of your personality type, and give you practical methods and advice on how to counteract any negative elements, and help you grow as a result.

3
Learn How to be More Socially Open

The first letter of the INTP personality trait is I for introversion.

An introverted person is not necessarily someone who is totally lacking in confidence and crippled by insecurity, and can actually be someone who is quietly confident, but finds it hard to mix. This could be for a number of reasons; it could be that you simply can't think of something to say, you don't connect well with strangers, or it can be that you simply need a little time to warm to someone, before you open up enough to show your true inner self.

Whatever your reason for being an introverted soul, the key to turning this into a major positive is to understand how to open up and be more social yourself.

Shyness is something which can be overcome, but it takes time and effort. The shyest people on the planet often feel like they have an affliction, and this can be a truth – shyness can stop you from taking opportunities, meeting people, and it can turn you into someone who is bitter and lonely, because you simply can't push yourself to speak and meet new connections, before you begin to blame yourself for it all. The answer? Understanding that shyness is something you can conquer.

As an INTP personality type, you are not someone who is totally crippled with shyness, but you do have it to a degree. You are someone who likes to think, someone who likes to explore a situation quietly, and that doesn't lend itself to long conversations with strangers. The thing is, those long conversations with strangers can actually be thrilling, and can open many a door, either in terms of relationships, friendships, work connections, or possible opportunities in life overall.

Social skills don't just include speaking however, they also include listening and this is something you can do very well indeed. What you need to learn to combine this with, is the confidence to simply open your mouth and speak, about anything!

So, how can you become a little more socially open?

Listen, pinpoint details, and speak

We have just mentioned that as an INTP, you are a fantastic listener, and you can use that skill to help yourself along a little. The next time you are in a social setting, perhaps at a party or in a meeting, and you are struggling to make yourself heard, simply because you don't feel confident enough to speak out, try listening first. Your observation skills are sharp, so watch people, check out their body language, listen to what they are saying with their mouths, and what they are saying with their bodies and perhaps their nervous habits. Are they fiddling with their hair? Are they tapping on the table? Are they looking around a lot, not able to focus on one spot? These are all signs that the person you are looking at is equally as shy as you, and this person is who you need to focus on.

Once you have used your observation skills to get the measure of them, simply start by making eye contact, and then give them a compliment. Everyone love a compliment! It could be about anything, their hair, their clothing, their shoes, their last piece of work, their taste in smartphone choice – anything. It really is that simple, and before you know it, said person will speak back to you, and

13

the slow conversation will pick up speed. Try this every single day, and before you know it, your social skills will be growing.

Never say 'no' to an invite

We say 'never', but try not to say 'no' too often at the very least. If you turn down too many invitations, you're simply not going to be asked to go out with friends or colleagues too often, and that isolates you socially, making the problem ten times worse. Simply say 'yes', and then see where the day or night takes you. As an INTP, you have a tendency to be spontaneous in terms of your decision making, so use that trait for a different means, and try and learn to go with the flow in social situations.

Take it in baby steps if you need to; you don't have to head out to big parties straight away, you can work up to that over time. Head out for coffee with a work colleague, venture to the cinema with a friend, try a workout class with a buddy, basically get yourself out and explore different social situations. You will soon see your confidence grow, and then as a result you will begin to open up and show your true self.

Consider the worst-case scenario for a second

We don't tend to recommend focusing on negatives as a habit, but for this particular scenario, focusing on a negative can actually turn out to be a positive. What is the worst that can happen if you speak out and no-one listen to you? Yes, it's embarrassing for a second, but did anyone die? No. Did the sky fall down? No. Will you get over it? Yes. Grab a drink and you'll be fine!

By thinking of the worst-case scenario just for a fleeting second, you can put your fears into perspective, and realize that it is very unlikely to even happen. By watching everyone else, you can see that at least one person says something and no-one listens, at least one person falls over on the dance floor, probably someone drops their food down their top whilst eating their meal – do they care? Probably a little, but they style it out, and that's what you need to learn to do.

You can't change yourself completely, and that means that you are unlikely to ever be the life and soul of the extroverted party and be happy about it; you are an INTP, and you should of course embrace that quiet confidence that you exude. What you need to do however, in order to grasp any potential opportunities that may arise during social gatherings or outings, is to learn how to be more comfortable in social situations. This doesn't have to mean you're speaking to everyone and dancing on tables, but it means that you don't feel too scared to speak, and once you arrive at that point, over time, you will feel much more at least as a result.

4

Learn How to be More Sensitive And in Touch With Your Emotions

An INTP is certainly not a cruel person, so leave that notion at the door. Instead, an INTP has the tendency to occasionally be a little too fact and logic focused, that they have a slight leaning towards saying something which may unintentionally hurt the feelings of someone who is much more emotionally focused instead.

As an INTP, have you ever been in an awkward situation where you found that something you said has upset someone else in your circle? You probably have, and whilst you probably never meant to cause offence (hopefully), you probably didn't realize you were saying anything wrong at the time.

The whole reason for this is that as an INTP, you are very focused on logic. You don't understand extreme emotions which are attached to situations. That's not to say you are lacking in feeling, far from it, but you are someone who is much more fact focused, and that means someone who makes a decision based on the feelings they have in their heart or soul, is something you don't totally understand. Instead, you prefer to explore the situation for a minute, think at a few solutions, and then go with the one that makes the most factual sense, and the one that is probably a little abstract but sure to succeed.

So, reasoning aside, that doesn't mean you shouldn't learn to be a little more considerate of the feelings of those around you when you are explaining a situation or issue.

You can do this by thinking before you speak, learning how to be at one with your own emotions, tapping into your intuition (and as an INTP you have a fantastic intuition), and by considering that there may be a more emotional answer to a problem, rather than a factual one.

Let's explore these one by one.

INTPs can be condescending and insensitive, so learn to think first and speak later

It sounds harsh, but you shouldn't take this as a criticism. The fact that you are so fact driven means that you are super-successful in terms of coming up with abstract solutions, but your failing is in your sensitivities.

When you are with someone who is a little more emotionally driven than you are, think for a second before you explain your side of the situation. How would you feel if someone was about to say what you really want to say? Would you be hurt? Upset? A bit annoyed? Learning to think before you open your mouth is a key skill in life, and one that can be used in various situations.

Your tendency to spontaneous actions is a key part of your personality make up, but learn to take a minute before speaking. Think of what you want to say, pause for a second, breathe, and word your statement in your mind before verbalizing it. By slowing down your thought process, you are much likely to be less condescending and more emotionally aware. You cannot take back what you have already said, even though at the time you probably didn't think you had said anything wrong, but taking a second can give you the time to salvage a situation before it happens.

Learning how to be at one with your own emotions

You are not an emotional-free person, you are actually quite sensitive yourself, but your logic often overrides your feelings. Your intuition is very strong, which we will talk about a little more in the next point, but you need to learn how to accept the fact it sometimes fact isn't always correct when it comes to solving a problem.

You are very able to think creatively and come up with solutions which others might not have thought of, but what is your gut feeling? It's really about imagining how something feels, rather than how it works.

The next time you are pondering the answer to something, take a little more time than you normally would. Yes, go through the logical side of things, because that is so easy for you to do, and it comes as second nature. Then, dare to delve into your emotional side. Is there a solution which your heart wants more than your head? What would happen if you went down that route instead? Talk to a friend and see what their take on it is. Allow yourself to feel and all yourself to validate those feelings as real.

Feelings are part of who we are as human beings, they enable us to be happy, sad, angry, joyful, jealous, excited, and help make life worth living. Tapping into your heart as well as your head is the way forward.

Tap into that strong intuition

As an INTP you have a great intuition and imagination, but at times you don't always trust it. Learning how to trust your intuition is something that will take time, but throwing caution to the wind is the way forward. This is all part and parcel of learning how to be at one with your emotions in many ways, because if something doesn't feel right in your gut, then the chances are that it isn't right.

A mother's intuition is not a myth, it is a strong feeling in the middle of the stomach, with roots head into the heart, which tell you whether you are in danger or whether you are safe, whether someone is to be trusted or whether you need to be cautious. It goes back to the days to the days of the cavemen, when the fight or flight response kept our hairy friends alive, and away from the clutches of predators. It is that strong feeling that you are okay, and as an INTP you are have a tendency to second guess that feeling.

As an experiment, ty going with your intuition just once. Ignore that logical side of your brain which is telling you that it doesn't make factual sense, and instead, just tune in on the way the situation and the options, and how they make you feel. Go with what your gut is telling you, and see what the outcome is. Learning to be balanced and to trust your instinct as well as your logic is the key to becoming a well-rounded human being, INTP or otherwise.

By following these tips, you can slowly begin to rein in some of your responses, learning to become more aware of the way that you may make people feeling, without intending to do so.

5
Learn How to Become More Organized and Present in The Moment

One of the most troublesome INTP weaknesses is being occasionally ... how can we put it? Scatty?

An INTP can be late, unorganized, and forgetful on occasion, which is the part of the rebellious side of the personality type. A dislike for rules and guidelines is the other side of it. You big rebel, you!

Now, the good news is that this is certainly one of the easiest traits to fix, because with a little time management training, you can ensure that your scattiness is reined in somewhat. Of course, that doesn't mean that your imaginative nature needs to be totally curtailed, but learning how to be organized in terms of your belongings, your work, and your time management skills, will certainly help you become more organized in life overall, and will help you open more opportunity doors in terms of work. You are also much less likely to annoy people when you are on time!

You would think that a personality type that is so focused on logic and analysis wouldn't have this problem, but a tendency for being unorganized is one of the biggest contradictions of the personality types overall!

So, how can you address this issue and become more organized overall?

Firstly, you need to identify which areas of life you have problems with. Are you late a lot? Do you forget things easily? Or, are you a combination of the two?

Get yourself into a routine

Do you have a habit of sleeping late and then losing half of the morning? Are you looking after yourself? It's important to get yourself into a routine that is regular, in order for your productivity to be at its potential. Being in a routine means that you are getting enough sleep, your body is getting the vitamins it needs from its food intake, and you are giving yourself 'me' time, which is just as important as work. Ironically, by doing this, you are helping yourself become more organized, because you're not going to be running as late all the time. It's not rocket science, and to conquer that INTP lateness trait, a routine is really all it takes.

Write lists

A key point in becoming more organized and learning about time management is about understanding what you have to do. It's easy to become overwhelmed with too many tasks, but most of them could be small and done within half an hour. By writing down everything you need to do, you can clear out your mind and leave yourself focused on getting the tasks done on time, rather than missing tasks, being late, and forgetting things. List writing is not for the over-organized, it is for those who want to get the most out of their time overall.

Prioritize your tasks

Another important part of becoming more organized is to prioritize. It's no good wasting time on tasks that aren't that pressing, when you should be focusing on the things that are more urgent. In terms of work, this means addressing the issues which have deadlines attached to them,

Prioritizing is easy and quite addictive once you get used to it, and it really ties in with listing making. Write down everything you need to do, highlight the things which are more urgent, e.g. the things which need to be done or paid for by a certain date, and number them in order of importance. From there, do the most important things first. Addressing the INTP trait of being unorganized can really be that simple!

Keep a notebook at the side of your bed and in your bag

Another item which many INTPs struggle with is an influx of ideas, which can often come all at the same time. A way around this, to stop your head getting clogged up with too many thoughts, which can then lead to burn out, is to keep a notebook either at the side of your bed or in your bag. If you want to go down the technological route, you could use the memo function on your smartphone or tablet.

Basically, whenever something pops into your mind, to avoid you becoming distracted by it, and worrying that you might forget (which, as an INTP, you might), simply write it down and then you can address it at a later date, i.e. in the morning when you have had enough sleep. This idea is also great for writing down those logical (or emotional, as you learn to tap into that side or yourself), creative answers to problems.

Organize what you need the night before

INTPs are forgetful, and that means you are likely to arrive for work, or some other engagement, without the things that you really need. Taking control of the situation is the only way around this, i.e. packing your bag for work the night before, making sure that you have everything that you're going to require for the day. This also works in a two-fold way, because it means you're going to have more time in the morning to get ready, therefore making sure that you're not late, which is another weakness of the INTP type.

Use a planner on your smartphone
Because your particular personality trait loves to dabble in a bit of technology from time to time, enjoying its logical make up, a good way to organize yourself and your time is to make use of the calendar or planner function on your smartphone. Set up alerts to ensure you don't forget where you're supposed to be, and have your alarm sound beforehand, just in case.

Learning how to be more organized is really about taking control of yourself and the situation. INTPs love to solve problems logically, so this really should call out to that side of your personality. Whilst you don't love the ideal of rules and regulations, you should also recognize the fact that in order to make a living, you're going to need to adhere to certain time management rules – this is a simple fact of life!

This should really be one of the easiest of the 'how to' methods we're talking about, because whilst as an INTP you do have organization skill issues, the local ways to fix them are well within your reach.

6

Learn How to be More Secure in Your Decisions

Nobody gets anywhere in life without making decisions; it's simply not possible to bob from day to day without making a choice of some kind. These decisions don't have to be massive, they can be as small as deciding whether to have coffee or tea in the morning, whether to drive to work or walk, or it could be something larger, such as whether to take a job or refuse it, whether to buy a house or stay in your rented home. The problem with the INTP personality type is that although they are great at problem solving, they are often at the mercy of questioning those decisions and forcing a delay in proceedings as a result.

Are you always confident in your choices? If you're nodding your head then you're simply not human. Every single one of us wonders whether we made the right choice or not about a certain situation in our lives, but the difference between this occasional issue and the state that an INTP can occasionally get themselves into, is that worrying about something from time to time is normal, but an INTP overthinks the whole thing.

Again, this might sound like a total contradiction, because if this is your personality type, you are a fantastic problem solver, someone who thinks creatively and outside the box. Yes, that's true, but that doesn't mean that you are always confident in your choice, and that lack of confidence, or slight hesitation, can be enough to make you think about it more than you should, question it more than you should, change your mind a few times, and delay the consequences or actions of the decision. By that time, you might have missed your chance on whatever you were trying to decide on.

Annoying, I'm sure you'll agree!

Whilst as an INTP personality type, you are very straight forward in your thinking, you're logical and you love to come up with imaginative solutions, you aren't the most confident in yourself. Your introverted nature means that you are quiet, and that means you think rather than speak a lot of the time. Overthinking is never a good thing, because by thinking about something too much, you often put obstacles where they don't need to be, and you create hurdles that were never there in the first place. So, how do you learn to accept the situation, decide on it, and then let it go?

Practice.

You are not someone who makes rash decisions, and you are not someone who doesn't think things through enough before making a choice. This is where confidence comes in. Because whilst we can state that quite categorically, knowing exactly your type of personality and traits, you need to believe it more than anything. When you believe this, when you have faith in your choices, you will learn to trust yourself and your decisions much more.

A lot of this is linked into our previous chapter of learning to trust and listen to your intuition. Your gut feeling will guide you to a large degree, and if you can learn to trust that, whilst also applying that fantastic logical and abstract thinking thing you have going on, then you are sure to make some fantastic and very positive decisions – you just need to learn to trust yourself first and foremost.

So, how do you do it?

A leap of faith.

It might sound like an insurmountable mountain, but learning to really trust yourself and your choices is a process which takes time. Despite that, it is also a process which will be extremely valuable to you in the future, because you will be free of the baggage that has held you back for so long. You won't be delaying your decisions and missing opportunities anymore, because you will know that you did all you could do at the time.

Try this the next time you're faced with a decision and you're questioning which option to go with;

- Grab a pen and paper and write down your options for solving the problem
- You will probably come up with logical answers first, so tap into that intuition and see if you feel anything about a certain route, e.g. does one feel more 'right' than another?
- Close your eyes, breathe, and go with the one that feels right
- Take action to put it into practice

Try it, and after time you will see that it feels less terrifying every single time, until it is second nature.

Another thing to do is think about the worst-case scenario, to really put it into practice. If you make a decision now what is the worst that can happen? You make the wrong choice? Remember that a wrong choice isn't always final, and there are often many opportunities to put it right. You are human and that means you have the free rein to make mistakes occasionally. The thing is, when you tap into your emotions and your higher self, you are rarely going to make the wrong decision anyway.

The ironic thing about becoming more secure in your decision making is that it really addresses several key points of the INTP personality type. For instance, by becoming more assured, you are learning to listen to your intuition, you are becoming more sensitive because you are listening to your emotions, ad you are becoming more productive because you are not delaying your decision making by going around the houses three times over. This is really a win-win situation.

7

Learn How to Combine Problem Solving and Your Imagination

As a highly intuitive and creative INTP personality type, you are very used to thinking of abstract and different ways to solve problems, but in order to make this work for you as much as possible, you need to really push it to the limits. This is a perk of your personality type, a strength that you need to really make use of. The danger however is not trusting yourself with said decisions, and taking too long to make them. Of course, we have just addressed that in our last chapter, so you need to make sure you really cover that in order to help yourself in reaching your decision-making potential.

This final practical chapter however is about a slightly different approach, it is about making sure that you harness your fantastic imagination, and really adapt it to making decisions in the most abstract and creative way. If you can combine what we have talked about so far, e.g. your emotional openness and trust in yourself, then this will really help you further.

So, how can you be totally creative with your decision making?

Be totally clear on the choice you need to make

Whilst making a creative decision, it is easy to lose sight of the actual choice you have in front of you. It can be all too easy to go off on a tangent, and then you are going down a totally different route to the one that you need. Be sure that you know all the information you can about the choice you need to make, write it all down if you must, and be as objective as possible. Having said that, remember that there are emotional elements to every decision, as well as logical ones too.

Who else is involved in the decision?

Remember that your INTP type means that you have the tendency to be a little insensitive from time to time, especially in this type of situation, and you could find yourself butting heads with others. If someone else is involved in the decision-making process, you need to sit down and brainstorm ideas together. Rein yourself in from making wide sweeping gestures at this point, it is about gathering information, in order to really think about an abstract or creative way to solve that problem. We know that you are great at this already, but do you just want to be average great, or super great? Of course, you want to be super great!

Are there any other factors you need to think about?

Is there a cost element involved? Do you need to seek permission from anyone? In order to have all the information to hand, to be whole in your choice, you have to consider outside influences. If there is cost involved, how much cost, and what is your budget to solve it?

What timescale do you have to decide?

This is the key point for your particular personality type, because we know from our chat so far that you have a tendency to think about it too much and waste a little time. Be clear in your time limit, and don't go over it. If at all possible, make sure that you come to a decision early.

What resources can you use?

Write a list of the thing you can use, as this will help you pull it all together and come up with your most creative answer to said quandary.

Putting it all together

This is where you really excel, but there are a few pitfalls you need to try and avoid. We obviously know he first one – don't overthink it! Trust your intuition at this stage, and think laterally. You are blessed with your creative mind, so get brainstorming and listen to what your gut is telling you. Trust your decision and make it.

Imagination is not for children who come up with stories to tell at school, it is for all of us to use to come up with interesting and different ways to solve problems. You are really well stocked in this department because your imagination is vital in your decision-making issues. Yes, you do sometimes think too much, and yes, you have a tendency to be a tad bit too logical, but these can be counteracted if you can learn to be more dream-like in your problem-solving efforts. Don't be afraid to be different, you have the tools at your disposal to make it work for you, and those around you.

8
Conclusion

How'd you feel at this point? The hopes are that you are feeling upbeat and positive about the advice and information we have given you, and you are much more enlightened about your particular personality type.

Carl Jung depicted the different personality types out of a huge amount of research, and the Myers Briggs Personality Test was designed to examine your answers to key questions, bringing you to a final personality type answer. It's worth noting that you should also read up on the other personality types, because you may find yourself mirrored in a few of them too. If you find yourself reading it and thinking 'hey, that's me' then take that advice, and incorporate it into your main type too. Nobody is streamlined into one particular pigeon hole, we are all different and we all display slightly different, subtle changes when it comes to our own personalities.

The point of identifying your dominant personality type however is to help you learn from the perceived weaknesses that you will display. From there, you can understand them, take the advice, and become more well-rounded as a result of what you have learnt. Of course, it's no good simply reading this book if you're not going to really put some time and effort into taking our advice.

Your strengths and weaknesses work together to make you the person that you are, but that doesn't mean that you can't work to better yourself by understanding them. Nobody is perfect, and you should never aim to be either – a perfect world would be a very boring world! What you should do however is accept that change is a good thing, and once you start at something from a different standpoint, you can find great truth and knowledge.

As an INTP personality type, you are a true thinker, someone who listens, takes everything in, and allows himself or herself to think outside of the box to answer questions, and create opportunities. You are a visionary, and that should never change. What do you need to thing about? Your delivery of words perhaps, a nurturing of your emotional attachment, and your relationship with your own intuition.

Learning to become more organized will give you a clearer headspace so work on these issues, and this s perhaps the easiest of all the tasks we have talked about. If you really want to become ahead of the game however, as an INTP, you need to really work on becoming at one with your emotions.

By becoming your own best friend, you can learn to stop second guessing yourself, you can be comfortable with how you feel about the choices you make, and you won't need to worry about any potential problems in terms of speaking in an insensitive manner to others, when you truly don't mean to offend. Your intuition and your emotions are so intrinsically linked, and if you can tap into their power, and combine it with your fantastically logical brain, your creative mind, and your abstract thought processes, well, you're really going to go places in this world of ours.

A word of advice ...

We have briefly touched upon this, but now we are at the end of our journey together into the INTP world, it's worth mentioning it again. Remember to read upon the other closely linked personality types too. As an introverted type, you are referred to as a logician, someone who seeks out sense and meaning, rather than emotion. By reading about the other introverted types, you may see a few traits or weaknesses that you can learn from too, to help you become an even more well-rounded individual.

Note from the author

Thank you for purchasing and reading this book. If you enjoyed it or found it useful then I'd really appreciate it if you would post a short review on Amazon. I do read all the reviews personally so that I can continually write what people are wanting.

If you'd like to leave a review then please visit the link below:

https://www.amazon.com/dp/B075V5BDY1

Thanks for your support and good luck!

Check Out My Other Books

Below you'll find some of my other books that are popular on Amazon and Kindle as well. Simply search the titles listed below on Amazon. Alternatively, you can visit my author page on Amazon to see other work written by me.

ENFP: Understand and Break Free From Your Own Limitations

INFP: Understand and Break Free From Your Own Limitations

ENFJ: Understand and Break Free From Your Own Limitations

INFJ: Understand and Break Free From Your Own Limitations

ENFP: INFP: ENFJ: INFJ: Understand and Break Free From Your Own Limitations – The Diplomat Bundle Series

OPTION B: F**K IT - How to Finally Take Control Of Your Life And Break Free From All Expectations. Live A Limitless, Fearless, Purpose Driven Life With Ultimate Freedom

24826184R00021

Printed in Great Britain
by Amazon